CAN
PEOPLE
really
CHANGE?

CAN PEOPLE
really
CHANGE?

13 lessons from
13 years as a therapist

EMILY ROMERO, LPC, SEP

Thank you for buying the physical copy of this book. If you're like me, you also love to listen to your books.

Don't worry, I got you.

Listen for free:

curiosityrising.com/changeaudio

advanced praise

I was captivated by Emily's story and her raw humanity in this poignant and at times even poetic exploration of change.

Though the content is deep and layered, Emily deconstructs therapy and presents it in such an accessible and fun way.

The best part ..

It is the exact opposite of a self-help book - which was so refreshing!

Rather than having to ask myself if the author's opinion resonated with me and having to sift through what is theirs and what is my own, I came away with a deeper sense of my OWN thoughts and opinions and a closer connection to MYSELF.

It's a beautiful thing to be in the presence of someone that is safely and lovingly connected to themselves. This is what Emily embodies through her WRITING!

A brilliant and rare skill!

-Kathie Hoffmann

For every courageous person who entered the sacred space of the therapy room with me.

disclaimer

The names, stories, clients, and situations described in this book are composites of many individuals, drawn from both my experience and my colleagues' experiences. They are not meant to represent any specific person or event. The details have been changed and fictionalized to ensure the privacy and confidentiality of all involved. Any resemblance to actual persons, living or dead, is not intentional.

This book is intended for general information purposes only. Any application of the material set forth is to be used at the reader's discretion and is their sole responsibility.

contents

Prologue   17

Introduction   19

Lesson #1: Medicine to One is Poison to Another.   25

Lesson #2: Therapy Works Best When You're Ready to be Radically Honest with Yourself.   31

Lesson #3: The #1 Reason People Got to Therapy.   37

Lesson #4: Talk Therapy Isn't Really About Talking.   43

Lesson #5: Watering Myself Down Isn't the Answer.   49

Lesson #6: Self-Awareness is a Prerequisite to Self-Trust.   55

Lesson #7: Go Slow; Get Curious.   61

Lesson #8: Spiritual Bypassing 101: "Everything Happens for a Reason."   67

Lesson #9: Be the Buffalo.   75

Lesson #10: We're All Complicated.   81

Lesson #11: Decisions Are Best Made Deliberately.   87

Lesson #12: When You Get a Chance to Do an Ending Well… Take It.   93

Lesson #13: Maybe Over-Explaining Yourself Isn't the Gift You Think It Is.   99

Acknowledgments   104

About the Author   106

BTS of the Therapist → Author Journey   108

The Cut Lessons   110

Gratitude   113

kintsugi

Japanese | 金継ぎ, lit. 'golden joinery' also known as
kintsukuroi | 金繕い, "golden repair" is the Japanese art of
repairing broken pottery by mending the areas of breakage
with lacquer and powdered gold. It treats breakage and repair
as part of the history of the object rather than something to
disguise. The aesthetic is sometimes described as one of
appreciating beauty that is "imperfect, impermanent, and
incomplete" in nature.

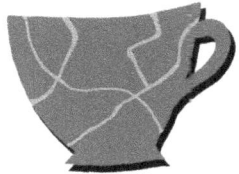

Kintsugi is inspired by the Japanese philosophy of *mushin*
(無心, "no mind"), which encompasses the acceptance of
change, fully existing within the moment, and fate as an
aspect of human life.

It's not about hiding the brokenness. But instead, illuminating
the reality of both the damage *and* repair that has occurred.

"We are all in this together and there is no therapist and no person immune to the inherent tragedies of existence."

*-**Irvin Yalom**, The Gift of Therapy*

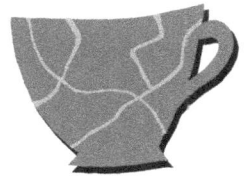

prologue

. . .

THERE'S a centuries-old belief that our core personality traits are predetermined and fixed throughout our lifetime.

Do you believe that?

Or, do you think it's possible for people to change?

To *really* change.

The deep down, *"I'm a new person"*, cellular-level-kind-of-change.

I was a somatic trauma therapist for over thirteen years. I spent tens of thousands of 50-minute sessions with hundreds of people from diverse walks of life. And they all had one thing in common. They all desired some kind of change in their lives. They were all coming to me because they needed *something* to be different.

But they were also stuck - stuck in the mud of hopelessness. An inner question would often emerge as we explored these muddy pits, wells, and liminal spaces they found themselves in.

"Is it even possible for people to change?"

And an even deeper question often waited underneath...

"Will it be worth it?"

As I transition to the next season of my life and my career as a therapist ends, I'm pulling back the curtain on therapy for you. I'm letting you in on one of the most unique relationships with some of the most incredible people - all attempting to conquer one of life's greatest challenges... change.

I'll share with you the lessons I learned as a therapist. Along with some of the wisdom I gained from being a space-holder for possibility and hope merchant for many. And finally, insights from being a professional secret keeper for your deepest desires, fears, and things you'd only say to someone bound by confidentiality.

At the end of it all, you can decide for yourself if you believe change is possible and if you think the juice could be worth the squeeze.

introduction

. . .

YOU DON'T HAVE to be a former therapist to understand the magnitude of big life transitions. They're timeless and universal thresholds we *all* experience. All throughout time and across cultures, people have come of age and navigated rituals through different seasons of life. Each of us will have plenty of opportunities to straddle these two worlds. Between what used to be and what's still to come. I've heard from many people how these bardos can be confusing, messy, and stressful. They often get disoriented at these intersections of life. And they're not necessarily wrong.

Change *can* be really hard.

But, here's something else that's also true:

Transitions are powerful portals for reflection.

Entering a new stage of life can be a ripe opportunity to deliberately choose your path forward and become *more* of who you really are. I like approaching big life transitions like the magical time warp they can be. After the goodbye but before the next hello. A void where words fall short. Yet, the *body* is clear.

After closing my private practice a few months ago, I've indulged in this **portal's reflective and liminal headspace**. Capitalizing on the medicine. I knew it was important for me to close loops on the past thirteen years. I wanted to honor the chapter of my life that was "being a therapist" instead of just plowing ahead to when everything makes sense again. **It's been disorienting to say the least.** Maybe even drifting into existential territory.

And.

It continues to be worth it.

Last year, I was given a firm knowing it was time to end my career after thirteen years in the therapist chair. It was technically late summer, but the color of the leaves outside tried to convince me it was already fall. Visually reminding me of the transient nature of life.

The specific clarity as to *why* this was the next right step didn't come included with the download. Apparently, there's some assembly required. I've become familiar with these death and rebirth cycles by now. Familiar enough to at least trust the inner wisdom when it arises, even if I can't make sense of it right away. **I've never found it helpful to overstay my welcome once the whisper only I can hear, comes through.**

So, with inner trust in tow, I began telling my clients that our work would end in just five months. And even though *I'm* comfortable acting on my intuitive pings without the full picture, I didn't love that I couldn't give them a satisfying answer when they understandably wanted to know why. It's only been in the reflecting and writing I've done recently that the deeper layers have begun to reveal themselves. Some, more surprising than others.

———

I developed a highly precise inner clock during my career as a therapist. I could accurately sense when the 50-minute hour was up. No watch required. It's a completely pointless skill now that I've decided to close this chapter. It's not even really a good party trick. Luckily, a highly specific internal stopwatch isn't the only thing I'm leaving eight years of agency work and five years of private practice with.

I'm also leaving with a ton of lessons, taught to me through well over ten thousand hours of sitting with people. Through hours of holding space for the deepest wells of sorrow and the seemingly endless paths of fear. Through hours of celebrating "little" wins that turn out to be, not so little at all. And through witnessing so many *other* people's…

Big. Life. Transitions.

And now, my gift to you…

Distilling down the thousands of hours and insights from hundreds of people navigating change.

Here are thirteen of my biggest lessons from thirteen years as a therapist.

*Now... come. Let's have some **tea**.*

*And talk about the **things.***

"If you want to keep growing, you may find that some belief, healing, or story that was freeing to you yesterday can enslave you today. Yesterday's truth can be today's lie."

- McCall Erickson, *The Second Half of the Mountain*

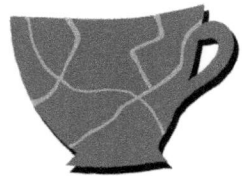

lesson #1: medicine to one is poison to another.

. . .

"Isn't this a red flag?!" Cassie asks as she looks at me with pleading eyes. I can't tell if the video froze or if she's found a way to not need to blink, through sheer will.

She'd just gotten done telling me about how her boyfriend of four years wants to discuss moving in together. After a lifetime of running from true intimacy, Cassie has spent the past two years excavating why a healthy relationship is so scary to her.

I flip through some of our previous conversations in my mind. Connecting this to her pattern of looking for any escape route she can find. We've done so much work together by this point, I don't even need to say anything. I just look at her, head slightly tilted to the right, lips pressed together in a faint smile. Encouraging her to connect with what she already knows. I can see it in her tentative eyes as the inconvenient truth further reveals itself. Her protective parts put down their armor.

She knows she wants to build a life with this man. She knows the scary and right answer, is to not run.

THIRTEEN YEARS as a therapist taught me some universal truths about how similar we all actually are. Simultaneously, I saw how unique and vastly different our life experiences can be. That's why prescriptive therapy doesn't work. What I said to my client at 8am might have been the exact reminder they needed to hear to take action. Three hours later though, in another session, if I shared the same perspective, it could reinforce an unhealthy pattern the person sitting in front of me was struggling with.

Medicine to one. Poison to another.

A growth edge for one person might be to leave a romantic relationship they've known for years isn't going anywhere. Instead of hoping that moving in together will wave a magic wand and solve their problems. While Cassie, on the other hand, needed something different.

Healing doesn't have a universal path. We all have different cycles to break.

And also, yesterday's medicine could be today's poison.

There's another layer of complexity to this. This is when discernment becomes a superpower. The exact same person will need different things at different times. And there can be a shadow side to anything. Take being a "reflective person."

Reflecting = Medicine... when it allows me to slow down and be intentional.

Sometimes, I need to make space for deep reflection to gain a better understanding of myself so that I can know what comes next. Early in my self-discovery journey, it was crucial to reflect on the life I'd lived and the experiences that had shaped me. Asking myself lots of questions helped me gain clarity about the life I wanted to live.

Reflecting = Poison... when it keeps me stuck in the life-force draining space of indecision.

Sometimes, all that reflecting bites me in the ass. Ruminating in my mind, second-guessing, overthinking, and replaying a conversation I had with a co-worker from eight years ago is often the last thing I need to do.

I need to get out of my head, into my body, and into my life.

"The most courageous things I've ever done began with simply telling the truth, even when the truth meant something would end."

- Alix Klingenberg

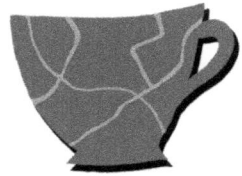

lesson #2: therapy works best when you're ready to be radically honest with yourself.

. . .

RADICAL HONESTY with yourself is not for the faint of heart. There are lots of good reasons people don't want to be *that* honest with themselves. It's usually based in survival and some sort of fear. If we're being really honest with ourselves, quite often, change is involved. I've found that once I know something, I can't *unknow* it.

"So, what brings you in?"

It's a question I've asked hundreds of times. Over the years, the responses have contained varying levels of self-awareness about the real reason someone is coming to therapy.

Sometimes the reasons are specific and clear. Often though, they're not. They just know they need something to be different. And then, some answers hint at an ultimatum from someone else.

Not much surprised me anymore. Until Andrea's answer.

She introduced me to a new pattern about to emerge, when she responded with..

"Well, I was scrolling on TikTok..."

It's been fascinating to witness therapy become "trendy" in the past few years. It's discussed in a very different light than when I first became a therapist. I've seen really positive impacts from this shift as therapy is becoming less stigmatized.

And.

I've also seen the pendulum swing too far. The watering down of nuanced concepts. The self-diagnosing, not only yourself but everyone around you. *(Narcissism is real. And not everyone you don't like is a narcissist.)* I've also seen "insights from therapy" be weaponized against people. And sometimes, enabling people to stay stuck. The exact opposite of therapy's intentions.

If you're going to therapy because it's "en vogue" or because someone else thinks it's what you "should" do, you're not likely going to reach its full potential. This doesn't necessarily mean it will be harmful. But the ceiling will be low until you're truly ready, to tell the truth about who you are and how your life became what it is. You could spin your wheels and spend your savings for decades without reaching your desired destination.

Radical Honesty can be one the hardest things to do. But if you want to get the most out of therapy I haven't found a path to reaching the fullest potential without taking the radically honest route.

I kept digging in with Andrea over the next few

months. Challenging her and asking questions that got us below the TikTok diagnoses. I sensed there was more than what she originally shared.

She wasn't intentionally hiding things from me. She was just still in the process of discovering them for herself. She had internal parts that protected her from knowing her deepest fears. Too scary to admit.

Does acknowledging them make them real?

As each new layer of honesty revealed itself, we crept closer to the real reason.

And when we finally reached the core of her fear, her eyes spontaneously filled with tears, "I think I might be broken... forever. No one could ever really love me."

I felt her truth in my body as she said it out loud.

That's enough Radical Honesty for today. Understanding where her fear came from in the first place, that can wait until next week.

I've had many opportunities throughout my career to pause and be Radically Honest with myself about my role as a therapist. Boundaries exist in the therapeutic relationship for good reasons. And I used all these reasons to justify why I landed on the "very firm" side of the spectrum of acceptable boundaries in the therapy dynamic. My "expert" status at dodging questions might've even been a running joke with clients. Who knows, maybe the word "fortress" was used. For many years though, I confidently stood behind my blank slate boundaries.

But life doesn't often let you stay on your high horse for too long. Just when you think you know something, the wind gets knocked out of you on the long fall from your pedestal.

I was brutally and beautifully shown the healing potential on the other side of a therapist embracing nuance. I experienced a therapist deliberately choosing to show up as a human first without letting the "therapist script" get in the way. Human to human connection. Human to human healing. I couldn't experience it without also getting curious about how I was showing up as a therapist. I had to begin questioning if such a starkly one directional relationship was still the kind of healing I wanted to be a part of.

Turns out, Radical Honesty isn't just crucial for the person seeking therapy. It's for all of us.

"A bird sitting on a tree is never afraid of the branch breaking because its trust is not on the branch but on its own wings."

- Charlie Wardle

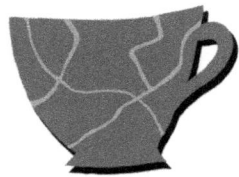

lesson #3: the #1 reason people go to therapy.

. . .

THE SPECIFIC WORDS I heard people use to describe the reason for beginning therapy always varied. However, I repeatedly heard about the desire for tools to manage anxiety and feeling overwhelmed. And often, people wanted to heal trauma from their past.

Many 'P' words were used: procrastination, people-pleasing, and perfectionism.

There were words to describe what seemed like individual concerns: insecurities, lack of coping skills, low self-worth, decision paralysis, and lack of confidence.

And there were words that captured the relational creatures we all are: difficulty setting boundaries, fear of abandonment, and intimacy issues.

The person sitting across from me just wanted help getting unstuck from whatever mud they were in.

During my final years as a therapist, I began digging below the specific words. I wanted to understand the essence of what people actually need.

Regardless of the answer to *"What brings you to therapy?"* the patterns were becoming clear. Even when the presenting problems seemed vastly different, I realized most people needed the same thing.

They need to trust themselves more.

Don't worry; the lesson here isn't a platitude like *"Just trust yourself!"* It's not that easy. I know that. You know that. I've spent years fleshing out how to *actually* build Self-Trust.

But what I witnessed was palpable. **The most profound healing I ever saw came on the other side of people learning they could trust themselves.**

"What would you do if you were me?"

Julie had just finished explaining to me the crossroads she found herself at.

She was about to get promoted again for the third time in seven years. But, she wanted to leave the secure career path she'd been on to follow a different dream. A dream with a lot less stability but, hopefully, more joy. She was feeling drained by all the back and forth happening in her mind and desperately wanted a life raft.

We're still in the early stages of our work together so she hasn't yet come to expect the unsatisfying answer I'm about to respond with. Soon, though, she'll be able to predict how I'll redirect questions like that back to her.

Reminding her, where the answers reside.

When you have more Self-Trust, you don't have to outsource your decisions. When you trust yourself, there is a deep knowing that you can handle whatever life throws at you, so you don't have to be in a constant state of worry. Even when you make mistakes or things don't go according to plan, your core trust in yourself doesn't waver.

Once I began working with people through this lens, I saw how this indirect approach to reaching their goals actually worked. We weren't laser focusing our efforts on "building confidence" or "feeling worthy". We weren't playing whack-a-mole with every crisis of the week. I was providing a framework for them to gradually and consistently build Self-Trust. And it was working.

They started to trust themselves more, and as the Self-Trust grew, they noticed they were getting closer to the original goals that brought them into therapy in the first place. They felt less anxious and better able to handle stressful situations. Their relationships improved. They were more confident with their boundaries and life decisions.

My favorite description of this is when Julie described the **"quiet confidence"** she felt after a year of taking this approach. It wasn't a "fake-it-till-you-make-it" confidence. She didn't "positive affirmation" her way there. It was real and genuine confidence emerging from within.

The kind of confidence that comes from more Self-Trust isn't contingent on the world being any certain way.

That's my favorite part about this approach. It's not a one-off solution. When you do the work to build Self-Trust, you create a solid fountain. It generalizes to other areas of your life. And you're prepared for the next time life inevitably throws "life" at you. When you have a strong sense of trust in yourself, you don't have to try to control everything around you.

Instead, you get to show up in your life and actually, live.

"In the arms of another nervous system, we become more of who we are meant to be."

*- **Deb Dana**, Polyvagal Exercises for Safety and Connection*

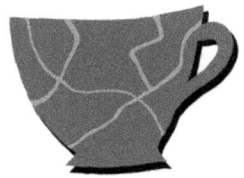

lesson #4: talk therapy isn't really about talking.

. . .

NOT TO OVERUSE AN ALREADY
OVERUSED metaphor, but talk therapy is a bit like
an iceberg. And believe it or not, the "talking" part is
just the tip. A bit ironic, given its name. It includes the
words we say, the philosophies and beliefs we explore,
the resources we cite, the perspectives we ponder, the
stories we share, and the insight we gain. We're...
talking. A fly on the wall would know we're "doing
therapy".

But almost 90% of an iceberg is underwater. If we only
focus on what's visible, if we only pay attention to the
words being spoken, we risk missing out on so much
more.

*It's Tuesday. Which means I see Missy at
9am. The spunky, purple-haired yoga teacher.
Halfway through our session, she has a
moment of clarity. Followed by a noticeable
relaxing of her shoulders and an audible exhale.*

*After a pause she looks up at me and
unknowingly describes the underwater part of
the iceberg when she says to me, "Ya know,
Emily... This has happened before. It's like
we're having a conversation but then
something else is happening too. Different from
the words we're saying. I understand things
more but it's almost like we're talking in code.*

It doesn't really make sense to my brain, though."

My response? "Yep, I totally get that."

And then I let her in on the secret. "Our nervous systems have been talking."

What's under the water doesn't rely on words. It relies on vibes and energy and all the things we don't hear when our nervous systems are communicating. It's when **I lend my regulated nervous system to the person sitting across from me**. I get to offer my regulation as a gift.

And when I'm at my best, that gift is steady, grounded, and present. Co-regulation can occur. By the end of the session, their system can experience more of their own regulation. And when they know how to regulate themselves, that's when the real "magic" happens.

As with anything, reps are necessary. It takes time to build capacity in their nervous system. Stability and consistency. That's what I get to share. Reliably offering an experience of co-regulation in each session. Also, underwater, I get to offer my "Self" energy to coax out their "Self" energy. And Self, doesn't require words.

Self is a calm, curious, connected, confident, and compassionate presence. The presence of Self alone can be healing and regulating. Once someone is able to experience their own Self energy and develop enough resiliency to reliably return to a regulated state, **they have a solid foundation to figure everything else out.** They can go inside for their answers. And trust what they find.

And yeah, sometimes, all this happened while we were "just talking".

"The privilege of a lifetime is to become who you truly are."

- Carl Jung

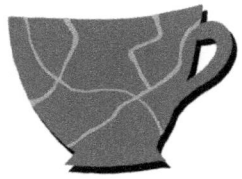

lesson #5: watering myself down isn't the answer.

. . .

It's a Sunday morning and I'm making my way through the produce section of the grocery store. I catch a glimpse of the woman on the other side of the avocados.

I instinctively looked down before the cautious double-take confirms, it's not Tara.

But then, the replay of our last session begins playing in my mind. The struggles she was having. The pain she was in. I take a breath to send her some love from afar. Energetically holding space for her brokenheartedness.

Then, I think about her self-deprecating tendencies. I chuckled a little to myself because I see myself in Tara often. Sometimes, this allows me to feel confident and really enjoy our work together.

Other times, I have to check myself. Remind myself her path isn't mine.

I've made my way to the dairy section still thinking about her. Then, it hits me. An epiphany. Insight about a perspective I can offer her. I think it will resonate. For many reasons, she's been struggling with the idea of motherhood. The indecision has been taking a toll on her.

I fight the urge to email her right away, but instead, eagerly await our next session.

IF YOU'VE EVER WONDERED if your therapist thinks about you outside of session, I think you have your answer.

The perspective I want to share with Tara begins to expand beyond just her. Still holding the eggs in my hand, I feel the tug to write about it.

I think to myself how this way of looking at motherhood and indecision could be valuable for others too. I want to write about my own experience in this space. Maybe I could write a blog post or include it in the next newsletter.

I put the eggs into the basket and click into my notes section. Letting my fingers type out the flurried epiphany. I feel my chest flutter as the words flow. This, feels right...

There's something about writing that keeps tugging at me. A soul nudge I can't get away from. I've been pushing myself to share more of my writing for the past couple of years. It's been a massive growth edge. The kind of edge where comfort is not prioritized.

After I finish typing in my notes section, I imagine sharing this insight with my email list. A ping of excitement was quickly followed by a drop in my stomach.

What would Tara think? She's the one who sparked the idea, but what I wrote became about me. She's in a different place, so how will it land for her?

Then, I remember Halle, and what she shared with me in session a few weeks ago. What I have to say doesn't make sense with her life. What if she takes it the wrong way?

And what about Claire, the woman I saw a few years ago. Glimpses of our sessions fill my mind. Her heartbreak. Her longing. Fuck, what if she reads the email? I don't even meet with her anymore so we can't talk it through if she does has feelings about it.

I probably just shouldn't send any of this. Yeah, there's a good chance someone I'm working with or have ever worked with, is going to misunderstand what I'm saying.

I can't do that to them. I can't send it.

The uncomfortable growth edge I've been exploring has reliably connected me with a familiar voice. The voice of Fear. The voice that tells me to stay small, stay hidden, and stay quiet. The voice that tells me I can't survive being misunderstood.

I want to write things that make people feel *big* things. *This* is a desire I have. But I also happen to have a ruthless filtering system inside. Keeping me from sharing anything too honest or too real. Eliminating sentences that could be misinterpreted and stories that require "too much" vulnerability. I've gotten skilled at watering myself down for the sake of "protecting" the people I work with. This isn't the kind of writing I want to do. I want to write about the nuance and complexity of life. I want to contradict myself in my writing if that's required to say what's true.

I can't do any of the writing I long to do if I'm typing on eggshells.

It's ironic. I spend so much time working with clients to take up space in *their* life. To expand into *their* bigness. Yet, here I am, letting Fear keep me small.

Oh snap, maybe there's an even bigger lesson here.

Maybe I should write about it...

"But if you travel far enough, one day you will recognize yourself coming down the road to meet yourself. And you will say - YES."

- Marion Woodman

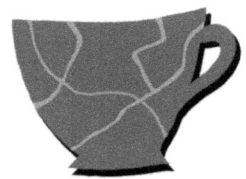

lesson #6: self awareness is a prerequisite to self-trust.

. . .

BUILDING on the premise that lack of Self-Trust is what fuels so many of the ailments we struggle with in modern society, let's dig deeper into a lesson on *how* to trust yourself more. Because we already established it's not as easy as the *Nike* slogan claims.

If you want to trust yourself more, you have to stop being a stranger to yourself.

Niki was a few months out from her divorce when she came to see me. She'd made it through the acute stages of grief after her wife moved out. She was done spending every night watching sappy movies and surviving on a diet of ice cream and Chinese take out - hoping for a "good" fortune cookie.

She was ready to re-engage with the world. Over the course of the first few sessions, it became clear to me how little Niki actually knew herself. So many of the answers she provided to my questions centered around her ex-wife. From where she had lived for the past decade, the things she did for fun, the clothes she wore, and even whether or not she liked to cook.

"So, what do you like to do?" I asked.

After a very pregnant pause she responded,

"Well, Vanessa loved it when I made dinner for us, so I used to do that a lot. Does that count?".

Niki is not unique. This was a struggle I saw time and time again from the therapist chair. And it was often followed by some version of the bewildered exclamation, *"Fuuuuuck, I don't even know who I am!"* It's a hard pill to swallow. And can be even more disorienting when you don't know where to start.

But this moment of Radical Honesty can be a catalyst for positive change. It allows you to have a beginner's mind. It can be an empowering part of the process, if you allow it to be.

Acknowledging that you don't know is the first step to knowing.

Because once you know that you don't know yourself, you can start deconstructing the choices you've made. You can take your life apart, and then put it back together in ways that make more sense.

"Wait, do I even like roller skating?"

Her eyes made it seem like she was pointing the question at me. But, without taking a breath, she continued, "I've been doing it for almost a decade. I made so many of my friends there, but I don't think I actually like it. What does that mean?!".

Niki's deconstruction process had predictably spiraled a bit in our recent sessions.

"This is so stupid; why does it even matter if I like tomatoes on my pasta?!"

This question actually was for me.

And so, I reminded her why we were doing all this work.

"Because every time you pause and ask yourself if you like something or not, no matter how mundane it seems, you have a chance to know yourself a little bit better."

And every time you know yourself better, you open the doors to trusting yourself more too.

I remind her, that we're never just talking about tomatoes.

Self-awareness isn't just for clients.

I saw how important this was as a therapist too. I had many opportunities in the first eight years of my career to try on different styles of therapy. I worked for a variety of different agencies with vastly different structures and priorities. I "tried on" other people's ways of doing things. I learned as much as I could from multiple supervisors and co-workers. I got to learn more about myself each time I made space for someone else's way of doing things. And so, when it was time to build my own practice, I knew *why* I was doing it the way I was.

The trust I had built in myself through knowing who I was as a therapist, served me well when I reached certain choice points in my practice. Like when I decided to refer a new client to a different therapist because their pain tapped into an experience that was still fresh in me. Or when I had to decide what was really sparking the desire to take a new training. Was it genuine interest... or just insecurity? And most pointedly, late last summer, when I knew it was time to end my therapy practice.

So much of it started simply by knowing who I am. And, allowing myself to change my mind.

I've learned even more about myself in the months since closing my practice. In fact, it appears that...

The layers of self-awareness are infinite.

"Blessed are the curious for they shall have adventures."

-Lovelle Drachman

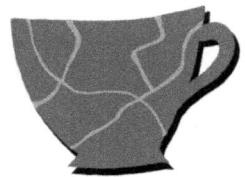

lesson #7: go slow; get curious.

. . .

Alex came to the agency I was working at specifically because it was a center for healing trauma. She must have recently learned about being Radically Honest with herself because she was ready to tell herself the truth about the "sexual experience" she had in college. It wasn't an experience. It was rape. And she was ready to deal with it.

She came into our first session, full steam ahead. During our intake session, she didn't show any emotion. Disconnected from her body, she quickly recited what had happened.

She confidently told me just how ready she was to process it and then "move on." She was used to efficiency in her life.

I was still in the first year of my career. Just an intern. My head still had the newborn smell.

I didn't yet know that the fastest way to process trauma is slowly.

So, I let her take the lead. I allowed her to guide us directly into the center of the trauma vortex.

THERE ARE many things I know now that I didn't know as a brand-new therapist. Titration might be the most important of them all. Titration is the somatic therapist's way of describing "little bits at a time" or "piece by piece." "One step at a time" or "as far as the headlights shine." Or, if we're talking about eating an elephant, "one bite at a time."

The metaphors to describe titration are abundant. And even if the metaphors don't realize it, they're all describing how to gradually build capacity in the nervous system. More capacity in the nervous system is what allows for your innate healing wisdom to emerge.

One way to define trauma is anything that overwhelms your ability to cope. **Anything that is too much, too soon, or too fast can be registered as a threat in your nervous system.** It can cause your system to go into a fight, flight, freeze, or fawn response. And the residue of that survival energy can get "stuck" in your system. This is what leads to being traumatized. (This, plus a lack of safe support afterward.) But not necessarily the event itself. This survival residue impacts your behaviors and decision making in unhelpful ways. Long after the original threat has passed.

This is why titration became foundational in how I approached trauma processing. Because even with the best intentions for healing, therapy that doesn't consider a slow and curious pace can be registered as traumatic in the nervous system. Remembering the past can feel like too much, too soon, or too fast, when it's not done intentionally.

You can't heal in the same nervous system state that you were traumatized in.

Trauma can't be processed quickly or solely in the brain. This is where titration comes in. Slowing things down, getting curious, getting into the body, introducing choice, and allowing space between drips are the antidotes to trauma symptoms.

If I knew then what I know now, my work with Alex would've looked very different. I would've clearly been able to explain the rationale for moving slowly and working around the edges of the trauma memory.

I would've been able to validate her desire to move fast and still have the confidence to set a slower pace.

I would've known that her wide, never-blinking eyes were a sign to slow down, even more. To spend time away from the trauma vortex. I would've asked her more questions about her dog. And the art she created. And the friends she loved.

We could've avoided overwhelming her system -

again. We could've avoided therapy also being "too much."

If I knew then what I know now, maybe, she would've even come back for a second session.

Going slow isn't my preferred pace most of the time. Just ask my 2x speed on Audible or anyone who's ever gone on a walk with me. It takes constant effort and continually reminding myself of the benefits of a deeper breath and a slower tempo.

But when I am able to apply this lesson, it's clear.

Life is just better.

"There is no such thing as a complete lack of order, only a design so vast it appears unrepetitive up close"

-Louise Erdrich

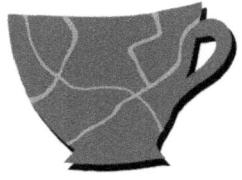

lesson #8: spiritual bypassing 101: "everything happens for a reason."

. . .

EARLY IN MY CAREER, it wasn't uncommon for me to hear the sentiment, *"Everything happens for a reason."* I heard other therapists talk about this push towards premature meaning making. I also saw this protective way of thinking play out within a client's support system. Many people are uncomfortable being in the messy unknowns of grief and loss. And if someone, therapist included, isn't able to sit with their own sorrow, hopelessness, fear, and shame, it's going to be nearly impossible to sit with someone else drowning in those gut-wrenching places.

This often leads to some well-intended attempts at "helping" with phrases such as *"Let's search for the gift to be found here"* or *"This is happening FOR you."*

And many unintentionally hurtful sentences that begin with, *"At least..."*

But after your world has been shattered in what should have been a mundane moment or you've spent your entire life scripted by unjust suffering, these platitudes often just inflict more harm than good. *Because they attempt to bypass what's real.*

And what's real is this: *Life can be cruel.*

Terribly unfair things happen every day. These platitudes try to talk their way around having to completely dissolve into grief, destruction, longing, resentment, and bitterness. They try to skip the "goo" stage of the chrysalis. These sentiments can also come from your own inner voice, based on long-ago indoctrinated beliefs. Or, naively hoping that if you can just find meaning in your wounds, maybe, it won't hurt so fucking much.

But arbitrary timelines don't work with grief.

It makes sense we want to move *out* of pain. There's a difference, though, between genuinely arriving at meaning after a windy and honest path and trying to convince yourself you actually believe the platitudes you're repeating. I've learned it's not about getting "through" these difficult emotions. It's about creating an intimate relationship with them.

So if you find yourself looking down at the floor covered with shattered pieces of your favorite mug, you don't have to try to hide the cracks or gaslight yourself into being thankful it broke.

Golden repair doesn't require gratitude for the breaking.

But you *can* choose to illuminate the reality of the cracks. Mending them with gold and beginning the next chapter of your life - deeply connected to the "both/and" nature of existence.

Because what's also just as real is this: Millions of people have turned their pain into purpose.

They kept going, even after each of their darkest days. They kept waking up, *especially* on the mornings it felt impossible. I myself live in the contradiction of believing everything I've written so far and also knowing how important meaning is. I've experienced the life-*giving* energy of full circle moments, synchronicities, and connecting the dots looking backwards.

I've felt inspired by the post-traumatic *growth* I've seen in the people I've worked with. It can be excruciatingly beautiful when someone alchemizes their pain into purpose. And, despite the pressure you may feel to turn everything into gold; you don't owe this to anyone.

It was five years into our work together when Logan said to me, with a slightly perplexed expression, "I think I might be genuinely grateful that sex was so painful and complicated all those years. I don't quite know how to put it into words yet, but it's actually starting to feel true."

She was still confused about how the thing she had carried so much shame about for her entire life was now morphing into something she was actually grateful for. Her mind hadn't fully caught up to the rest of her.

But it made a lot of sense to me. From the person with the outside perspective and access *to the details of the long journey she'd been on with her body.*

She had spent years working through the physical, mental, and emotional layers that come with painful sex before we even started working together.

And in our time, I got to witness how she learned to release trauma from her body, had honest conversations with herself and partners, advocated for herself with doctors, mothered all her younger parts, and began having a loving relationship with her body.

Her inner monologue continued, "Maybe... I actually do get it, but it just sounds cliche. If I hadn't gone through all of that, all the hopeless nights, I wouldn't have tried so hard to have the life I have now. I wouldn't know myself and my body the way that I do. And I probably never would've met Markus."

She finished her thought where the lesson began, "Maybe it did all happened for a reason."

Whether or not something happened for a bigger purpose isn't mine to decide for someone else. It's not my job as their therapist or friend or partner or funeral attendee to tell them the "reason" their world was destroyed.

"Making meaning" out of your darkest moments doesn't usually make for a great goal.

But it *can be* a really beautiful byproduct of doing the soul-wrenching work to heal.

"Not everything that is faced can be changed, but nothing can be changed until it is faced."

- James Baldwin

lesson #9: be the buffalo.

. . .

COWS AND BUFFALO can both sense when a rainstorm is coming. But their reaction to the storm is strikingly different. Once the cow senses the storm approaching, they will run in the opposite direction. Being that cows aren't very fast, it doesn't take long for the storm to catch them. And then, they keep running *with* the storm as it moves. So, they end up being stuck in the pain and suffering of the storm for a long time.

Longer than necessary.

Anyone who's ever tried to outrun an emotion, understands this.

Buffalo on the other hand, run in a different direction. Once they sense the storm, they charge *towards* it. They experience the exact same rainstorm as the cows, but since they run directly at it, they are able to make it through the turbulence and discomfort much quicker.

I used to move through the world like a cow.

Specifically when it came to difficult conversations and potential conflict, I'd do anything to avoid an uncomfortable talk with someone in my life. Often having to push down what was true for me or abandon parts of myself to "keep the peace." I know there were times this bled into my work as a therapist. Moments where it was "easier" not to push back on something my client said. Even though I knew a different perspective could be helpful in the long run. I avoided the temporary discomfort of their initial reaction.

Going towards the hard thing to eliminate extended suffering makes sense as a concept. But it's oh so very hard to put into practice when you've been a cow your entire life. Knowing a thing and doing the thing are vastly different.

As I started to become a buffalo, I had to do it in stages. Remembering titration. I practiced having difficult conversations, first, in relationships where it felt safe to do so. The path was often bumpy. And I messed up a lot. But I knew I didn't want to brush things under the rug anymore. I didn't want to go back. I also optimistically believed there were benefits to getting uncomfortable, on purpose. The further I went down the path, **the closer to my integrity I found myself**.

To the surprise of all my past selves, **on the other side of uncomfortable conversations was actually deeper connection and intimacy.** The exact opposite of what Fear told me would happen.

Trust isn't just built in happy and supportive moments. Deeply rooted trust actually forms during the discomfort of real and honest conversations. It's strengthened when we go through challenging times together. Running from hard conversations actually keeps us from the closeness and intimacy we crave.

Even with all the "difficult conversations practice" I'd had, my stomach was still in knots as I prepared for my session with Brynn. The session that only I knew would be our last.

There are infinite reasons a client/therapist relationship might not be a good fit, but this specific one - isn't my story to tell.

I'd spent weeks mulling it over in my mind. Imagining different ways the conversation could unfold.

Sometimes, I visualized the way I hoped it would go, holding onto the truth that I knew it was for the best. But often, letting Fear creep in with the "worst case scenario," trying to convince me I was abandoning her. But I knew what I needed to do. And I couldn't unknow it.

So, our session began, "Brynn, we need to talk..."

Have you ever repeatedly learned a lesson you wish *wasn't* true? Yeah, me too. I often wish having the hard conversation wasn't the answer. It's the simple, but not at all easy, path I can't seem to get away from. The path I know is required and worth it to live the life I want.

The path of the buffalo.

"We are each a multiplicity of parts, but we also have a Self that is compassionate and wise... When people become accepting and loving towards all their parts, those parts relax and become less extreme, and people feel more balanced, confident, and curious about their inner worlds."

*- **Richard Schwartz**, Internal Family Systems Therapy*

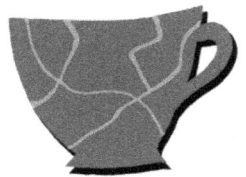

lesson #10: we're all complicated.

. . .

MULTIPLE PARTS of myself have shown up as I've been writing these lessons. And often, they don't agree. There's a familiar part of me that wants to give you a long list of disclaimers with each one. This part tries to convince me that being misunderstood is existential. This part is used to making my decisions, so she's not super welcoming to another part that has shown up more recently. Because this new part… she's *really* over giving disclaimers.

I would ask you if this sounds familiar or if you've ever had conflicting parts inside, too, but I already know the answer.

When I first described to Dylan how multifaceted we all are, I could see the recognition in her eyes immediately. It was as if I finally put words to something she already had a deep cellular understanding of.

It was a "well, duh" moment.

The language we used was just catching up to the complexity she already knew about herself.

Still, I reassured her there wasn't anything wrong with her. She didn't have "multiple personalities". She just happened to have an entire family of parts inside her. Just like we all do.

"Oh, this is so sweet... I feel so tender now towards this little girl in me." Dylan had one hand on her heart as the other quickly brushed away a tear.

Once she had a framework to visualize what used to feel so complicated, compassion for herself emerged spontaneously. Our work continued for many months, mapping out all the different parts she had inside. Some parts were young and vulnerable. Other parts were protective and vigilant. She noticed it was easy to genuinely like a few of the parts. At the same time, harsh judgment was still the initial reaction to some.

Once she had a pretty complete picture of all her parts, she described to me the image that had formed in her mind.

"So, we're all in a boardroom. They're all at this long table. Each one of them has a seat. Some of them are booster seats, but still, they're all there. And I'm at the head of the table. Standing up, listening to all of them. I'm the one running the meeting."

See how similar we all are?

We're all the same, because we're all complicated. But we're all complicated in very different ways.

While this complexity is beautiful and interesting, it can also be confusing. It can be tempting to think things would be easier if everything *was* simpler.

Suppose there *wasn't* a boardroom full of chatty inner parts. If everyone could nicely fit into a box. If people were in fact, all good or all bad. If things actually were all or nothing. This or that. Black or white. But I'm not just here to tell you about the infinite shades of gray that exist.

I'm also here to remind you that it can be black *and* white.

Things aren't as mutually exclusive as they feel.

Knowing this is true though, doesn't make it easy. Especially when things are polarized externally *and* internally. It can be easy to start to "should" all over yourself. *"I should feel happy about this..."* or *"I shouldn't have empathy for this person..."*.

The therapy container can be one of the few places where the messy and conflicting feelings are actually embraced. A space where paradox isn't feared. You don't have to choose between your joy or your outage to be accepted.

All parts of you are welcome.

And, when you begin to have understanding for all of who *you* are, it's hard to stop that compassion from rippling into the rest of the world.

"These mountains that you are carrying, you were only supposed to climb."

- *Najwa Zebian*, *Mind Platter*

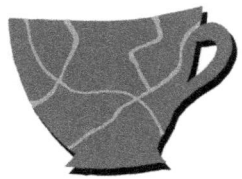

**lesson #11: decisions are
best made deliberately.**
. . .

UNTIL WE BRING the unconscious to the conscious, we're not actually as in charge of our decisions as we think. As much as possible, I want to make my decisions consciously.

Intentionally.

Deliberately.

I really want to know *why* I'm doing the things I'm doing.

There are many examples from my time as a therapist that would drive this lesson home. Stories of people I worked with who also wanted to be more intentional with their lives. Moments when we explored the life-scripts they'd been handed and how they were able to go off-script. Times when earlier lessons of Radical Honesty and self-awareness collided.

But as I sit and reflect on this now, I keep returning to the same memory. Or rather, a series of recent memories from my own life…

> It took a few weeks to be able to tell all of my clients about my decision to stop being a therapist. Even though the conversations about the end would continue for months, there was a sense of relief when at least everyone knew.
>
> I noticed I was comfortable sharing certain

aspects of why I was leaving, but not everything. Maybe it was because I still didn't fully understand it all myself. Or maybe the "blank slate" scripts were still trying to make my decisions.

Being a therapist hadn't just been a single chapter in my life. There was an entire book on my shelf dedicated to it.

It took me off guard last summer when I realized I was getting to the end of the book. The back cover sneaking up on me. I couldn't unsee the difference between the amount of pages on the left and the very few remaining on the right.

Without being able to fully grasp why the book had to end, I was left in limbo.

While the "in-between" spaces in life don't scare me nearly as much anymore, eventually, I would like out of this bardo. I am eager to know what comes next.

And, if I want more clarity about what the next book is, I need to better understand why a thirteen-year career I loved needed to end. And what better way to understand an ending than to revisit the beginning.

"How deliberate was my decision to become a therapist?"

"Which parts of me chose this career path?"

I'd be lying if I told you the answers to these questions revealed that I was always self-aware and intentional in my decision-making.

Because the honest answer to the first question is, "Not very."

And the second question illuminated many confronting answers.

As I sat with a mug of tea and a blank page to reflect on how I got to where I am, I was surprised. I discovered that not all the reasons I became a therapist were conscious. And it's only been since ending my practice that I've been able to really connect the dots.

The more I shined the flashlight around, the more I realized the multi-layered reasons for closing the therapy book were intricately intertwined with the inner work I'd been doing for decades.

Being deliberate doesn't mean you have all the answers.

Just because you slow down and ask yourself some tough questions, doesn't mean you'll automatically be granted access to all the levels of self-awareness. My hunch is, the infinite layer design - isn't an accident.

Sometimes, you have to leap for the net to actually appear. You can be deliberate in your decisions, based on the information you have at the time. And still trust yourself to build the parachute on the way down. It's not a leap of faith though.

It's a leap of trust.

You can make deliberate choices *and* trust yourself to figure out what you don't know yet. You can trust your body is telling you something for a reason. You can trust your '*no*' before you have access to your '*yes*'.

I took the leap of trust to end my career, without fully knowing why.

Taking that action, plus postmortem reflection, eventually illuminated the kind of healing spaces I *do* want to be a part of moving forward. I have clarity now about aspects of what I want next in my career, but that doesn't mean I have all the details figured out. Far from it. I'm continuing to deliberately step into the unknown. And I'm up for the challenge of living my life in this nuanced place. I'm anticipating it will be messy and complicated at times.

But it's okay. Because I trust myself.

"Doing one thing differently is very often the same as doing everything differently."

-Matt Haig, *The Midnight Library*

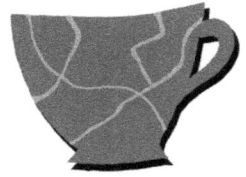

lesson #12: when you get a chance to do an ending well... take it.

. . .

ENDINGS ARE IMPORTANT. When it's possible to do them well, you should. I know, I know… therapists aren't supposed to say "should." But hey, I'm not a therapist anymore. And I'm okay contradicting myself in order to say what's true.

Every moment, things all around us are ending. It's inevitable that everything will change, evolve, and ultimately, end. Death is a constant reminder. Some of these endings are really scary and painful. Sometimes they crack us open in unimaginable ways that we can't fathom ever coming out on the other side. And sometimes, these endings are just really uncomfortable and would require a difficult conversation. So, we avoid them.

Putting blinders on doesn't prevent change from happening.

But this doesn't stop many of us from channeling our "inner cow". We often try to resist change because of how uncomfortable we imagine it will be. We avoid acknowledging that it's even happening. Or we deploy the "cut and run" strategy that Cassie so desperately wanted to be the answer.

We don't always get a choice over when or how things end.

Unexpected death blasted my world apart a few years ago. Nothing in my life was untouched. Being self-aware about my affinity for reflective headspaces still didn't prepare me for the existential overthinking that came with my dark night of the soul journey.

Every thought, feeling, belief, relationship, and decision I'd ever made was called into question. My role as a therapist definitely wasn't off-limits. I questioned my "blank slate" appearance and no longer accepted my familiar justifications for never self-disclosing. I knew I wanted to be more human with my clients.

Proximity to death propelled me to explore my aliveness. And it thrust me into being more intentional with endings.

It's possible to have endings that honor what was.

The lack of choice in that ending, forced me to look at the endings where I *could* have some say. And it completely changed the way I wanted to approach them. I started to actually believe that endings could be a fertile ground for growth and necessary evolution. That I had a chance to rewrite the script on what endings mean. That endings could be kind. And that endings could actually honor what was. Those are the kind of endings I want to be a part of now.

Even so, as I approached the final pages in the therapy book, the trap of resisting change was as tempting as ever. But I knew I could cause a lot of stealthy damage if I lied to myself about wanting to continue in the therapist role. I knew my clients would've felt the impact of those lies, even if they weren't able to articulate it. This was an ending I *did* have a choice in. And I wanted to do it well. I wanted to honor the sacred relationships I'd been a part of. I wanted to do the past thirteen years justice.

I've been through hundreds of final sessions in my career. They're often celebratory. A chance to revisit the words said in our first appointment together. We get to remember the reason they came to therapy in the first place.

And sometimes, we laugh about how the work became so much more than just, "I want tools to manage my anxiety."

I get to share my memories of our time together. And the progress I've seen that they may have minimized. We connect a lot of dots. These sessions are usually the definition of bittersweet.

But my final session with Shay is different.

It's not just a final session for her, with the reminder that if anything comes up in life, she can always reach back out.

This is an ending for both of us. This is the final goodbye.

I'm more honest with her in those final 50 minutes together than I have been in five years. I don't redirect her to herself and tell her, "It was all you!" when she shares how impactful our work together has been and her appreciation for me.

I actually take in what she says.

And I reciprocate, when I tell her how proud I am of her. I tell her truth - that I adore her. I tell her that she's also impacted me. And that I will genuinely miss seeing her.

It feels good to be that honest.

When the internal clock lets me know our time is done, we both stand up. And she asks for one more aspect of humanity, that I willingly give...

"Can I have a hug goodbye?"

"Good things, when short, are twice as good."

-Baltasar Gracián, *The Art of Worldly Wisdom*

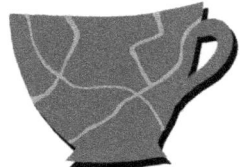

lesson #13: maybe over-explaining yourself isn't the gift you think it is.

. . .

"Shit!!"

My mug just broke into pieces all over the floor of my Airbnb apartment. Aka, my nomadic therapist office. It's right before a string of back-to-back sessions and I just lost my caffeinated pep talk.

More upsetting though, is the realization that the shattered mug on the floor is the mug that's more than just a mug. Tears try to break free from my eyes.

Grief has a pervasive way of attaching to inanimate objects that I find both incredibly annoying and sentimentally soothing.

Ugh. I "shake it off" (literally) and mentally prepare myself for someone else's problems. My stuff can wait.

Fast forward three years...

I pulled out the bottom drawer to restock my tea. And I see them. All my broken pieces. Hidden away. Exiled to the dark corners. Apparently, I can't get rid of them. But they're not useful, and anyone who sees them will tell me to throw them away. They're shattered after all.

I tried kintsugi once before. I'd bought a kit and set aside time to make the gold repair a ritual. I'd talked to enough clients about this metaphor for healing. I saw it work for other people. Maybe it could help me too?

Nope. Didn't go great. I think I even made it worse. The handle is defiantly not structurally sound now. I was flooded with disappointment and the belief that "healing stuff" only works for other people.

But when I see the broken pieces now, all these years later, I feel a new flutter of possibility. Dare I even say, hope? I'm different than I was before. I know what didn't work.

Maybe I can learn from my mistakes and try again.

Maybe there isn't a timeline for healing.

DOES THAT MAKE SENSE?

Because I really want to make sure you get what I'm saying...

Maybe I can explain it in a different way...

You know I'm talking about more than just a mug here, right?...

Wait a second, nope, I'm not doing that. I remind myself, once again, of the final lesson.

Don't take fifteen minutes to say what you could say in one sentence.

Give your clients (and readers) credit. *They get it.*

There's a good chance this will be the lesson I'm forever in the process of learning. I've never been accused of being concise.

But hey, I kept this one short. Maybe progress is possible.

Maybe people car change.

acknowledgements

With immense gratitude and reverence, I want to thank a few people who made this all possible…

First and foremost, Taylor. Thank you for sharing with me what you saw in my writing and for pushing me to give it a longer shelf life. Without you as my hype-man, I would not have just published a freaking book. 🐅 And without your ruthless editing, there would be at least six confusing and interwoven lessons in each of these 13 lessons… and way more self-deprecating commentary.

To my inner circle and the *Behind-the-Scenes* crew, for reading early drafts and cheering me on whenever Fear, Doubt, the voice who constantly repeated "*No one cares!*" were loud. Especially Kathie and Journey.

To J and C - thank you for joining me in early morning writing sessions, thank you for your patience in my early morning writing sessions, and thank you for inspiring the major life pivot that became the catalyst for this book. Without you, I wouldn't have known this book was in me.

As an outsider to the writing and publishing world, I want to thank Shannon, Dottie, and Cara for your unexpected guidance and support in a foreign space.

To all the authors (especially the reluctant ones) who paved the path of Self-publishing. The ones who came before me and wore down the gatekeepers so we can all publish the stories on our heart, in our own timeline. And for the IFS perspective to know that we can all publish a book from the energy of our "Capital S" - Self.

And finally, to those who this book is dedicated. Every single person who entered my therapy office and revealed a tender part of themselves to me. Words don't do justice to the gratitude, hope, and awe I feel when I reflect on 13+ years of these relationships. I hope you're also able to liberate yourself by doing whatever your soul is calling you to do.

about the author

Emily began her career as a therapist in 2010 and founded her private practice, *Curiosity Rising,* in 2019. With a passion for holistic and integrative approaches, she specialized in working with  complex trauma and anxiety through the lens of somatics, parts work, and psychedelic therapy.

She's the creator of *The Self-Trust Model*™ A framework designed to empower women to overcome self-doubt, overthinking, and insecurity so they can feel confident chasing their big dreams. She now leads training and certification programs. You can also learn more about the model on her podcast, *The Self-Trust Podcast,* and in her book, *You Can Trust Yourself.*

Formerly a proud nomad, Emily now finds solace in home and family amidst the beauty of Colorado. Whether she's hiking in the mountains or forest, it's always after a few tea lattes. Learn more about current offerings from Emily at: **www.curiosityrising.com**

bts of the therapist →
author journey

Emily turned to writing as a salve during the most challenging time of her life. It became a compass through dark nights of the soul and a bridge to what truly mattered. It led her on a journey of leaving her dream job as a therapist in private practice to pursue her soul's relentless calling. Giving herself permission to pivot when she heard the whispers.

You can join the movement behind-the-scenes, and witness the evolution from a soul nudge to a published author. Emily pulls back the curtain on the writing, editing, and publishing process.

If you've ever had a dream living inside you… this space is for you. When one person liberates her soul by sharing the stories in her heart; it's contagious. *Join BTS:* https://curiosityrising.substack.com/

the cut lessons:

- Someone Else Would've Had 13 Completely Different Lessons.
- The Antidotes to Grief and Trauma are Different.
- Being Misunderstood Isn't Existential.
- Know When to Pivot & When to Follow Through.
- Forgiveness isn't the Goal... it's a Byproduct of Healing.
- When Possible, Be Kind to Your Future Self.
- Self-Trust isn't About Becoming an Island.
- Disclaimer: I'm Done Giving Disclaimers.
- Healing isn't Linear.
- Nice Doesn't Equal Kind.
- It's Okay to Change Your Mind.
- Discernment is a Process and a Superpower.
- Not Every Person You Love is Meant to Be in Your Life Forever.
- Things Aren't as Mutually Exclusive as They Feel.
- Trusting Yourself Sometimes Means Breaking Your Own Heart.
- Sometimes Growth Feels Like Breaking.

- There's a Difference Between Lonely and Alone.
- Commitments Work Best When Made From Self.
- "All Seasons" Relationships Are Rare - Cherish Them.

secret bonus chapter

Still want more?

Check out a bonus lesson I only learned AFTER
leaving my dream career.

www.curiosityrising.com/secret

dear reader,

Thank you so much for reading my first book…

I'd love to hear from you!

If you gotten anything from this book, please, please, please… **leave an honest review** wherever you purchased this book. They help these lessons reach more people. Share you favorite lesson!

with curiosity,
emily